Domenico Scarlatti

100 Sonatas

in Three Volumes

Edited by

Eiji Hashimoto

Volume 3

Edition 3531

Volume 1—Edition 3529
Volume 2—Edition 3530
Volume 3—Edition 3531

G. SCHIRMER, Inc.

DISTRIBUTED BY

HAL•LEONARD®
CORPORATION
7777 W. BLUEMOUND RD. P.O. BOX 13819 MILWAUKEE, WI 53213

These three volumes, containing one hundred sonatas, are respectfully dedicated to the great harpsichordist, Mr. Ralph Kirkpatrick, who led me originally into the field of harpsichord with his imaginative and disciplined method, and who has given me, on this occasion, generous assistance, without which this edition would have been impossible.

Reg. No. 48669c

CONTENTS

Volume Three

		Page
Facsimiles		4
Domenico Scarlatti		5
Sources and Editorial Policy		7
Sonata 68 (K. 445, L. 385) in F Major		10
Sonata 69 (K. 446, L. 433) in F Major		14
Sonata 70 (K. 447, L. 294) in F♯ Minor		16
Sonata 71 (K. 448, L. 485) in F♯ Minor		20
Sonata 72 (K. 454, L. 184) in G Major		24
Sonata 73 (K. 455, L. 209) in G Major		28
Sonata 74 (K. 466, L. 118) in F Minor		32
Sonata 75 (K. 467, L. 476) in F Minor		36
Sonata 76 (K. 468, L. 226) in F Major		40
Sonata 77 (K. 469, L. 431) in F Major		44
Sonata 78 (K. 474, L. 203) in E♭ Major		48
Sonata 79 (K. 475, L. 220) in E♭ Major		52
Sonata 80 (K. 478, L. 12) in D Major		56
Sonata 81 (K. 479, L. Suppl. 16) in D Major		60
Sonata 82 (K. 485, L. 153) in C Major		64
Sonata 83 (K. 486, L. 455) in C Major		67
Sonata 84 (K. 487, L. 205) in C Major		72
Sonata 85 (K. 497, L. 146) in B Minor		76
Sonata 86 (K. 498, L. 350) in B Minor		80
Sonata 87 (K. 499, L. 193) in A Major		84
Sonata 88 (K. 500, L. 492) in A Major		88
Sonata 89 (K. 511, L. 314) in D Major		92
Sonata 90 (K. 512, L. 339) in D Major		96
Sonata 91 (K. 520, L. 86) in G Major		100
Sonata 92 (K. 521, L. 408) in G Major		104
Sonata 93 (K. 526, L. 456) in C Minor		108
Sonata 94 (K. 527, L. 458) in C Major		112
Sonata 95 (K. 532, L. 223) in A Minor		116
Sonata 96 (K. 533, L. 395) in A Major		120
Sonata 97 (K. 546, L. 312) in G Minor		124
Sonata 98 (K. 547, L. Suppl. 28) in G Major		128
Sonata 99 (K. 550, L. Suppl. 42) in B♭ Major		132
Sonata 100 (K. 551, L. 396) in B♭ Major		136
Notes on the Text of the Sonatas		140

4

Sonata 77 (K.469) in Venice XI 16

Sonata 91 (K.520) in Parma XV 7

DOMENICO SCARLATTI

Domenico Scarlatti, one of the most original composers of all time, was born in Naples in 1685 (the very year in which J. S. Bach and G. F. Handel were born). As was typical of a child born into a musical family of the time, Scarlatti was surrounded by music from his infancy, and received early musical education. He showed considerable talent before reaching the age of ten. As he matured, he was particularly fluent on the harpsichord, and his phenomenal technical agility became widely known. Since his father Alessandro was a famous composer of operas and cantatas, however, it was only natural for the young Domenico to begin to compose in these genres. While such works may have had some success at the time, they really did not reveal the exceptional genius that he later demonstrated in his keyboard works. Upon leaving Naples in 1705, Scarlatti worked in such cities as Venice and Rome, and in 1719 went to Lisbon as *maestro di cappella* at the Royal Chapel and tutor to Princess Maria Barbara, daughter of King João V. Although he returned to Italy on several occasions during his stay in Portugal, when the Princess married Prince Fernando of Spain in 1729, Domenico accompanied her to Spain, where he was to remain until his death in 1757. It was during this period of his life that his keyboard writing came into full bloom.

The first publication of his sonatas appeared in 1738, when he was fifty-three, under the title of *Essercizi per Gravicembalo,* and was followed by the Roseingrave edition of forty-two sonatas, published in London in 1739 (the latter entitled suites). There were numerous additional publications in the mid to late eighteenth century, but these mostly concentrated on his few early sonatas, while his later ones, musically more mature, were left almost entirely in manuscript. Ralph Kirkpatrick concludes that more than half of Scarlatti's 555 extant sonatas were written in the last five years of his life and that most of them were probably written for Maria Barbara. This leads us to believe that she too had great dexterity at the keyboard.

After Scarlatti's death, his name was known mostly through those early sonatas published in the eighteenth century. The other sonatas, left in manuscript, were little recognized until Carl Czerny made a partial edition in 1839, and Alessandro Longo revived nearly all of the sonatas in 1906, an edition which has since become very popular. As significant a contribution as this was, however, Longo somehow failed to present the true Scarlatti as revealed in the manuscripts, making insertions and alterations without much explanation. Kirkpatrick, nearly half a century later, culminated over ten years of exhaustive research with his book *Domenico Scarlatti* (Princeton University Press, 1953), together with *Sixty Selected Sonatas,* published by G. Schirmer. Kirkpatrick reached another milestone in 1972 when a complete facsimile edition of Scarlatti's sonatas, based mostly on the Parma manuscript, was published under his supervision and with his preface (Johnson Reprint Corporation, New York).

Performing Scarlatti's Sonatas

Scarlatti was the most outstanding keyboard composer Italy produced after Frescobaldi. The uninhibited, audacious, and flowing nature of his writing suggests that his sonatas were probably not composed at the desk through hours of assiduous planning and excruciating effort, but were rather written down as the result of his musical inspiration as it came through his fingers onto the keys. Such a theory would enable us to make a further conjecture, that there must have been other pieces improvised but somehow never notated and thus not preserved for later generations.

Scarlatti's sonatas reveal an extraordinary and original technique and highly idiomatic writing, in which the maximum effect and capability of the instrument were explored. They are hence parallel to Chopin's piano or Paganini's violin works. Interestingly enough, Scarlatti's absolute command of and total dedication to his instrument made it possible for him to transfer to and express on the harpsichord idioms and effects of various other instruments. These too became essential ingredients of his expressive technique. As Kirkpatrick puts it,

> The imaginary orchestration of harpsichord sound is seldom absent from Scarlatti's thinking. In this imaginary orchestration there are endless possibilities for shift of solo instruments, for changes of accompaniment color, for alternations of groups of instruments or varying sizes and color—in short, for all the resources of the eighteenth-century classical orchestra, strings, woodwind, brass, and percussion, as well as the castanets, mandolins, and guitars of Mediterranean popular music.
>
> *(Domenico Scarlatti,* Chapter XII)

Scarlatti's writing is not a display of strict counterpoint; rather, voices are quite freely treated. At times, one voice may branch out into several; at other times, multivoices are squeezed into one; and in these processes voice leading does not necessarily follow the conventional manner—a leading tone or a dissonance might be doubled, a dissonance might be introduced suddenly without preparation, or a note of suspension might drop out without going into its resolution. Since the harpsichord, unlike the piano, cannot produce dynamic changes by varying finger touches, Scarlatti sought to accomplish this by thickening or thinning the texture. The effects are reinforced by broadening or contracting the range of the voices. *Acciac-caturas* (tone clusters) and wide leaps also are important elements in special and often breathtaking effects for accent, crispness, and drive. In repetitions of a phrase, subtle changes of color and nuance are brought forth by the exploration of different registers, octave doubling, and/or slight alteration of notes; further, a phrase may not be repeated the expected number of times and, exceeding our expectations, produces surprise and freshness. As eventful and rich in content as each sonata is, however, it is tightly woven, and this makes his genius even more outstanding.

Scarlatti does not seem to have left any specific instructions for fingering, except the sporadic indications *Mutandi i deti* (change fingers) on repeated notes—but he does not say which fingers—and *Con dedo solo* (glissando)—in only a very few instances. He was, nonetheless, quite fastidious about the distribution of the hands, and there are numerous places where we find *D (Destra*—Right) and *M (Manca*—Left). Sometimes these indications appear to be rather unorthodox and deliberately difficult, and thus the temptation might arise to rearrange the hand distribution for the sake of security and facility. Indeed, some modern editions have done so. But while accuracy of notes may be more easily attained by such rearrangement, the dramatic excitement, dazzling effects, and rhythmic intrigue skillfully created by the original hand distribution will then be so minimized that the performance will have no excitement or glamour.

Unlike many of his contemporaries who wrote for the keyboard, Scarlatti did not indicate arpeggiation by signs. Does this mean that chords should always be struck simultaneously? On the guitar and mandolin, whose sound Scarlatti adopted on the harpsichord, arpeggio playing is a very essential technique and is used constantly, regardless of whether the chords are written that way or not. If a slowly arpeggiated chord evokes tender expressiveness, a fast one generates accent and intensity. On the harpsichord as well this is one of the important means of expression, particularly in the practice of improvisation and recitative accompaniment. Bearing this in mind, then, one should not jump to the conclusion in playing Scarlatti's sonatas that chords are always to be struck simultaneously just because there is no indication to arpeggiate them. One must extract and supplement the true meaning of the music behind the written notes. After all, how could one project the passionate strumming of the Spanish guitar that Scarlatti created on the harpsichord without adopting arpeggio playing? Yet one must also guard against exaggerated indulgence in this effect, remembering that any practice, if it is excessive and mannered, loses its fresh meaning and becomes monotonous.

Quick and frequent shifts between major and minor keys in a sonata as if to illustrate the sun shining, then moving under the clouds; rests or fermatas followed by the sudden appearance of unexpected materials in the most unexpected keys; unsettled harmonic wandering suggesting infinite goals, and intricacy of progressions; violent and percussive rhythm; hauntingly beautiful melodies—all of these vividly reflect Scarlatti's emotions and background, cultivated and refined in the Mediterranean peninsulas. These characteristics make his music an interesting contrast to Bach's, which usually pursues one particular affection in a movement or a piece. In performing Scarlatti's sonatas, therefore, one must be able to interpret quick changes of temperament as though one were an outstanding actor.

Scarlatti's sonatas are often regarded as single-movement structures, each one independent of the others. The truth is, however, that the majority of them are paired in the original sources. This was not uncommon among his Italian contemporaries, such as Francesco Durante, Domenico Paradisi, Domenico Alberti, and later the Abbate Lorenzo de Rossi, Antonio Sacchini, Luigi Cherubini, etc., all of whom wrote two-movement sonatas. Most of Scarlatti's earlier sonatas are single, independent ones, but from Venice I (or, around K. 150) on, the majority are grouped as pairs of sonatas in the same or parallel keys. There are approximately 390 sonatas which fall into such a paired arrangement. In addition, there are some which are grouped three sonatas to a set—examples of this kind include Sonatas 61, 62, 63 and 82, 83, 84 in the present edition. In the case of the sonatas *da chiesa* or *da camera* by Bach, Handel, Vivaldi, etc., certain tempi, meters, or forms are fundamental bases for the layout and order of movements, but in Scarlatti's sonatas, pairs are so diverse in assortment that there does not seem to be any such system. Some are a combination of two contrasting characters, such as slow and fast, simple and complex, sorrowful and jubilant, and/or common meter and triple; others are more or less the same in character, as though complementing each other. In any case, the paired arrangement is evident in the manuscripts; therefore, to convey accurately Scarlatti's character and expressiveness, one should always approach the performance of the sonatas with complete respect and care for these and other clues to the composer's true artistic intention.

Cincinnati, Ohio   Eiji Hashimoto

Sources

These one hundred sonatas are drawn from a printed edition and several manuscripts of the time, the earliest extant sources, as no keyboard autographs by Scarlatti can now be found.

1. ESSERCIZI

ESSERCIZI PER GRAVICEMBALO / di / Don Domenico Scarlatti / Cavaliero di S. GIACOMO e Maestro / dè / SERENISSIMI PRENCIPE e PRENCIPESSA / delle Asturie &c.

This collection of sonatas (K. 1–30), published in 1738, probably in London, was dedicated to King João V of Portugal. It is a beautifully engraved edition. The modern facsimile of this collection is available from Gregg Press Limited (London, 1967).

2. VENICE

At the Biblioteca Nazionale Marciana in Venice are fifteen manuscript volumes, containing 496 sonatas (MSS 9770–9784). They were probably copied in Spain for Queen Maria Barbara and are one of two most important sources, the other being the Parma manuscript. Volumes I through XIII consist of thirty sonatas each (except Volume X, which has thirty-four sonatas), and they are dated as follows: Volumes I–II, 1752; III–VI, 1753; VII–IX, 1754; X, 1755; XI–XII 1756; and XIII, 1757. The other two volumes, unnumbered, are each in a different hand from that of Volumes I–XIII. They contain sixty-one and forty-one sonatas and are dated 1742 and 1749, respectively. Kirkpatrick numbers the former XIV and the latter XV.

3. PARMA

Another fifteen volumes, containing 463 sonatas, are preserved at the Biblioteca Palatina, Sezione Musicale (AG 31406–31420), in the Conservatorio Arrigo Boito in Parma. They too were copied in Spain and are dated from 1752 to 1757 (Volumes I–V, 1752; VI–VIII, 1753; IX–XI, 1754; XII, 1755; XIII–XIV, 1756; and XV, 1757). Most of them duplicate the Venice manuscript, and the handwriting of both is quite similar. From Parma XIII (Venice XI) on, even the sonata numbers coincide. Parma XV, however, contains forty-two sonatas, of which the last twelve (K. 544–555) are missing from Venice XIII.

4. WORGAN

This manuscript, which was once owned by Dr. John Worgan, is now in the British Museum (Add. 31553). The forty-four sonatas contained in it are mostly duplicates of Venice XIV and XV.

5. MÜNSTER

Five volumes, containing 349 sonatas, in the Bischöfliche Santini-Bibliothek (Sant. Hs. 3964–3968) in Münster, were once owned by a collector of eighteenth-century music, the Abbate Fortunato Santini (1778-1862).

Aside from these, there are other manuscripts, including one housed in the Fitzwilliam Museum in Cambridge (twenty-four sonatas) and another in the Bibliothek der Gesellschaft der Musikfreunde in Vienna (seven volumes, 308 sonatas), but they are of less significance than those indicated above and thus have not been used in the present edition.

Editorial Policy

1. For the majority of the sonatas appearing here, I have referred to the Venice and Parma manuscripts, both of which are usually quite legible. Since their handwriting is so similar, it makes one wonder if they were copied from the same source, possibly by the same copyist. In some places both manuscripts contain identical and what seem to be obvious mistakes, which may have resulted from mistakes made in the original. In making the present edition, I have added an explanation in each of these instances unless there are discrepancies between the two manuscripts where one is logical and the other is not, in which case I have chosen the former without comment. If there is true uncertainty as to which one is justified, I have given both versions at the end of the volume so that the reader will have the option of drawing his own conclusion. A note in parentheses (♩) means that it is my interpretive addition and is actually absent in the sources.

2. Reflecting the common practice of the period, an accidental in the sources generally applies only to the note immediately following (unless the note is repeated on the same pitch, even across a bar line). This means that accidentals were usually written each time they occurred, even within a bar, and unless a note is immediately preceded by an accidental, it should be interpreted as a natural, even though the previous note of the same pitch in the bar may have a sharp or flat. Unfortunately, however, this basic rule is far from consistent. There are cases where accidentals were taken for granted or where cancelling signs of various kinds (mostly ♮, though sometimes ♭ is used to cancel ♯, or ♯ to cancel ♭) may appear as a warning. In deciphering such passages, one must rely on his musical judgment, verified by parallel or similar passages or inferred from stylistic understanding. In questionable places, I have added comments. Naturally, my application of accidentals in this edition is consistent with our modern system, i. e.

an accidental applies to all the notes of the same pitch until the end of the bar. Small accidentals above or below notes are my editorial supplements.

3. For editorial ties I have used dotted lines instead of regular ties. Slurs between appoggiaturas and their main notes are not always present in the sources, but I have left them exactly as they appear. In case these slurs are present in one manuscript but not in the other, I have included them.

4. Little attention seems to have been given in the sources to keeping the right-hand part on the upper staff and the left-hand part on the lower. As the treble and bass clefs are fixed in the upper and lower staves respectively, when both hands are engaged in a higher or lower range, all the parts are placed on one staff, while the other is left blank. (Only Sonatas 8 and 19 are exceptions, since they switch to various clefs—soprano, alto, and tenor, as well as treble and bass.) To facilitate reading I have changed the clefs of staves as necessary, so that the right-hand part would always be on the upper staff and the left-hand part on the lower. Unless the designation of hands is specified, the distribution has been made at my own discretion. On the other hand, to preserve the clarity of some arpeggios and scales or to avoid unnecessarily complex shifting from one clef to another on a staff, I have retained the original system. When a part is silent, rests have been added, unless they would create confusion or unless both hands are placed on one staff. Needless to say, indications of *D (Destra)* and *M (Manca)* have been strictly respected; but *D* has been translated to *R* (Right hand) and *M* to *L* (Left hand). If one hand crossing over the other makes reading difficult, I have adopted a three-staff system.

5. Vertically aligned notes in the sources are usually stemmed individually, which creates congestion in the limited space (Example 1).

Example 1

Sonata No.3
Kirkpatrick 24
Essercizi 24

Sonata No.50
Kirkpatrick 347
Parma IX 20

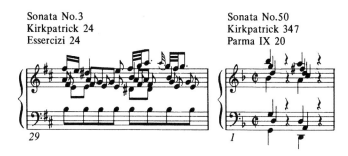

I have made the stemming more consistent, as follows: When more than two voices are present on each staff, the outermost voices have been stemmed separately, and the inner voices of each hand have been stemmed together (Example 2).

Example 2

As for horizontal division, eighth or sixteenth notes having arbitrarily placed flags like ♪♪♪♪ or ♪♫♫ have been beamed together according to rhythmic and metric units: ♫♫♫ . If notes are grouped ♫ ♩ ♫ in 6/8 meter, they have been altered to read ♫♫♫ ♫♫♫ , and ♩.♩. has become ♩. .

6. As a relic of modal notation, a key signature in Baroque music often contains one sharp or one flat less than the number expected today. That is, G minor might have only one flat at the beginning while E♭ is treated as an accidental throughout the piece. Examples of this in the present edition include Sonatas Nos. 3, 5, 6, 9, 12, 13, 16, 17, 21, 25, 26, 30, and 33 in the first volume (Sonatas Nos. 12 and 13 of the Parma manuscript have the complete number of sharps); Nos. 46 to 57 in the second volume; and Nos. 74, 75, 78, 79, 93, and 97 in the third volume. There are numerous examples of key-signature changes in the middle of a sonata, and some of these are also one short of the normal number of sharps or flats. I have modernized them all. While the double-sharp sign, 𝄪 , is only infrequently found (No. 42, Parma and Venice), at other times a sharp is added to a note already sharped by the key signature (Nos. 4, 38, 46, etc.) or, for example, simply G♮ or D♮ is indicated in lieu of F𝄪 or C𝄪 (Nos. 39, 47, and 54). In all of the instances I have used 𝄪 . In certain key contexts, I have also changed B♮, C♮, or F♮ to the enharmonic spellings of C♭, B♯, or E♯.

7. First and second endings at the repeats are quite ambiguously and loosely indicated in the sources. There might be slurs above and below the staves (⌒⌣), the sign :‖ might be placed in the middle of the bar, or at times no specific signs at all are used. I have replaced all of these varying indications with the modern system of ⌐1.⌐ ⌐2.⌐ . If the last bar, even when balanced by an incomplete opening bar, lacks the full number of beats, I have supplied rests.

The occasional appearance of slurs above and below the staves of first-half endings is often puzzling. Examples of these are particularly abundant in the third volume of the present edition. While some of them are to be interpreted as ⌐1.⌐ ⌐2.⌐ , as I have mentioned, there are others which cannot be appropriately interpreted in this way. Especially if such slurs occur in only one of the two principal manuscripts, Venice or Parma, their significance seems to be considerably diminished. Kirkpatrick interprets them as calligraphic decoration, and there is certainly enough justification for this interpretation. Or they could possibly serve the same function as the indication *Volti,* which reminds the reader that the sonata is not complete, but continues on the next page. In any case, in this edition, I have pointed out all of these instances at the end of each volume.

I have kept the corona signs (⌢) which appear almost always above and below the final double bar lines of sonatas (occasionally at the end of the first half as well) in the Venice and Parma manuscripts. Although it would be logical to assume that they suggest a prolongation of the final notes (or rests), they are sometimes found above and below the final notes themselves as well, and neither the *Essercizi* nor the Worgan manuscript (with one exception) gives them at the final bar line. In the latter, the word *Finis* almost always appears at the final bar line, though coronas sometimes occur above or below the final notes as well. It is therefore more likely that the coronas were meant merely as an indication of an ending, and whether the last note ought to be held longer or not should be determined from the musical context rather than exclusively from the existence or absence of coronas.

8. At the conclusion of the first halves of sonatas (which always come at a page turn) in almost all the sources (including the *Essercizi*), there appears the indication *Volti* (turn), *Volti subito* (turn immediately), *Volti presto,* or an abbreviation like *Vti. pto.* I have omitted all of these indications.

9. Aside from what we find in the Roseingrave edition, Scarlatti's use of signs for ornaments was rather restricted. The trill was the only type that he seems to have intended, but the signs *tr* and *w* appear quite indiscriminately. For example, while the Parma manuscript shows *w* , the Venice manuscript in the corresponding place might have *tr* or vice versa; or similar passages or sequences within the same manuscript use both *w* and *tr* , etc. It is therefore almost certain that these two signs mean the same thing. In fact, some scribbled *tr*'s are hard to distinguish from the sign *w* . I could have chosen only one of these signs for all the trills, but my desire to be as faithful to the original as possible has persuaded me to leave them as they are. All the sonatas in the *Essercizi* use the single sign *m* (for *w*), while in Worgan the sign *tr* is found throughout. As for the Venice and Parma manuscripts, although the two signs coincide most of the time, discrepancies occasionally arise. That is, in Venice, Volumes XIV and XV, *tr* predominates, but from Volume I on the appearance of *w* gradually increases and eventually predominates. In Parma, on the other hand, *w* is more consistent, but Volume II displays an arbitrary use of the two

signs. Ornament signs within parentheses are my editorial supplements.

Tremulo (or *Tremolo*) was used so broadly and loosely in the seventeenth and eighteenth centuries that it could mean rapid reiteration of one note or quick alternation between two notes in various ways, depending on the circumstance. Scarlatti's meaning of *Tremulo* (*Tre., Trem. Trem^lo*), although nowhere defined, seems to be synonymous with that of *tr* (trill), as there are a few cases in which *Tremulo* is used interchangeably with *tr* in parallel passages. *Tremulo,* however, seems to apply more to long notes than to short ones.

Some eighteenth-century composers, such as F. Couperin and C.P.E. Bach, notated accidentals within ornaments, but others took them for granted. In the sources of Scarlatti's sonatas, no accidentals are attached to ornaments, nor have I added any in the present edition, such as 𝄫𝄐 for ♯♮ , because that the trill occurs between *f♮"* and *e♭"* rather than between *f♯"* and *e♭"* is obvious. Similarly, it is also evident that [music example] equals [music example]

10. There are various note values used in the appoggiaturas in the sources (♩, ♪, ♪, ♪, ♪ , etc.). The choice of them seems to have had little to do with their actual length, since different appoggiaturas occur in similar passages in the same sonata, or in exactly the same place in different manuscripts. The relation of these appoggiaturas to their main notes is also rather inconsistent. As in the case of ornaments, I have faithfully copied them as they are in the sources, and if there are discrepancies among the manuscripts, I have so indicated.

11. The figure 3 to indicate triplets is frequently absent, or only sporadically used. I have added it the first few times when triplets appear.

12. If the notation happens to be rhythmically inaccurate, I have revised it and made an explanatory comment. There are, however, numerous cases of ♩. ♪♪ and ♩. ♪♪ which, imprecise as they are, were rather common at the time, and I have thus retained them.

13. Spellings of tempo indications are not always consistent or the same as modern spellings, but they have been kept exactly as they appear in the sources.

14. The pitch indications used in the "Notes on the Text of the Sonatas" are as follows:

C_1 C c c' c" c'''

Kirkpatrick 445
Venice X 28, Parma XII 24
Longo 385

Allegro, o presto

68

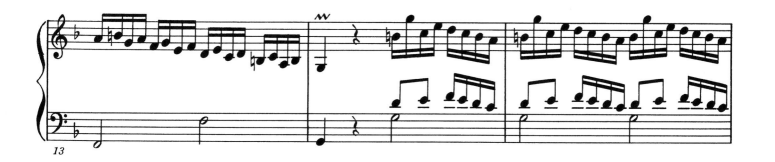

14

Kirkpatrick 446
Venice X 29, Parma XII 25
Longo 433

Pastorale
Allegrissimo

69

Kirkpatrick 447
Venice X 30, Parma XII 26
Longo   294

Kirkpatrick 448
Venice X 31, Parma XII 27
Longo 485

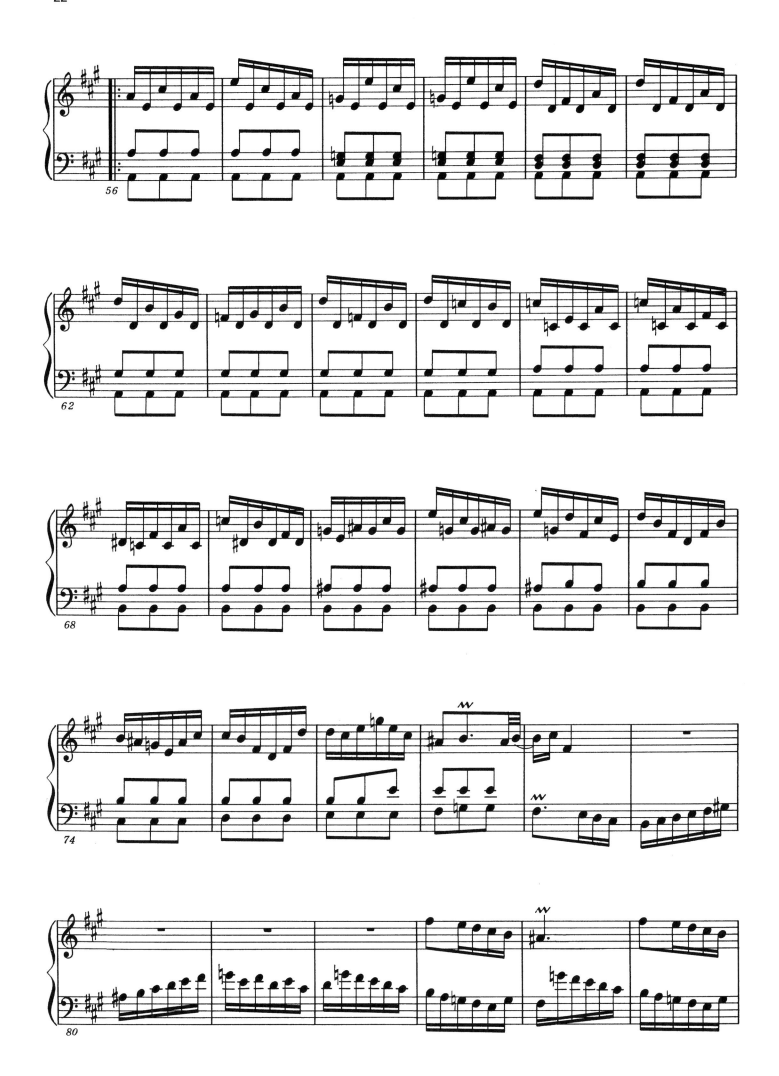

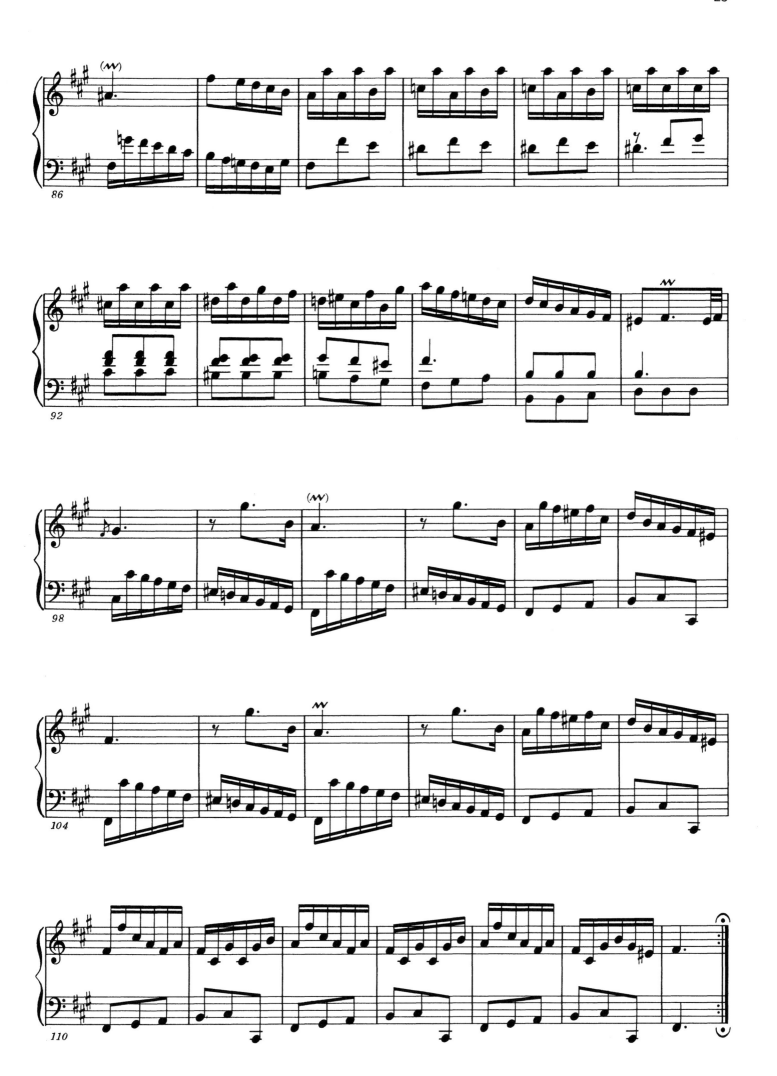

24

Kirkpatrick 454
Venice XI 1, Parma XIII 1
Longo 184

Kirkpatrick 455
Venice XI 2, Parma XIII 2
Longo 209

Allegro

73

32

Kirkpatrick 466
Venice XI 13, Parma XIII 13
Longo 118

Andante moderato

74

36

Kirkpatrick 467
Venice XI 14, Parma XIII 14
Longo 476

Allegrissimo

75

Kirkpatrick 468
Venice XI 15, Parma XIII 15
Longo 226

Allegro

76

con deto solo

44

Kirkpatrick 469
Venice XI 16, Parma XIII 16
Longo 431

Allegro molto

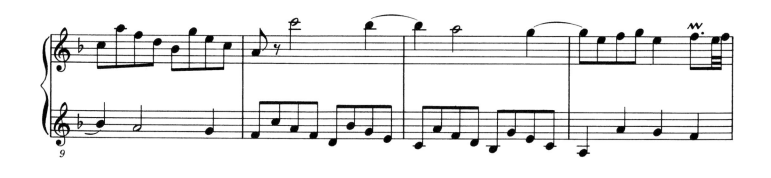

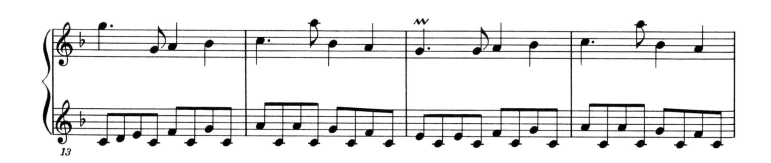

39

43

47

51

56

48

Kirkpatrick 475
Venice XI 22, Parma XIII 22
Longo 220

Allegrissimo

79

51

55

59

63

67

Kirkpatrick 478
Venice XI 25, Parma XIII 25
Longo 12

Andante è cantabbile

80

58

Kirkpatrick 479
Venice XI 26, Parma XIII 26
Longo Suppl. 16

Allegrissimo

81

62

Kirkpatrick 485
Venice XII 2, Parma XIV 2
Longo 153

Andante è cantabile

Kirkpatrick· 486
Venice XII 3, Parma XIV 3
Longo 455

Kirkpatrick 487
Venice XII 4, Parma XIV 4
Longo 205

76

Kirkpatrick 497
Venice XII 14, Parma XIV 14
Longo 146

Allegro

85

80

Kirkpatrick 498
Venice XII 15, Parma XIV 15
Longo 350

Allegro

Kirkpatrick 499
Venice XII 16, Parma XIV 16
Longo 193

Kirkpatrick 500
Venice XII 17, Parma XIV 17
Longo 492

Kirkpatrick 511
Venice XII 28, Parma XIV 28
Longo 314

Allegro

89

47

50

53

56

59

96

Kirkpatrick 512
Venice XII 29, Parma XIV 29
Longo 339

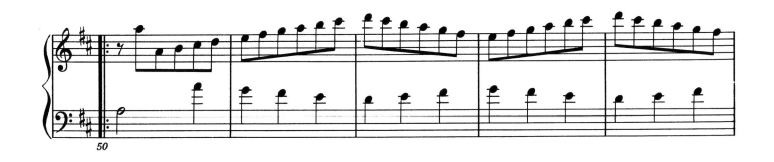

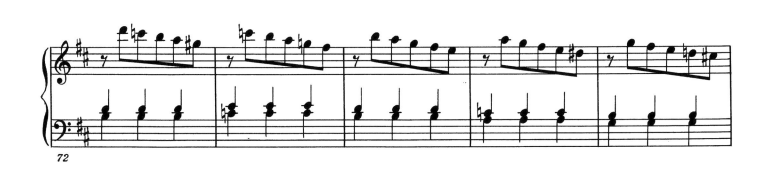

Kirkpatrick 520
Venice XIII 7, Parma XV 7
Longo 86

Allegretto

91

Kirkpatrick 521
Venice XIII 8, Parma XV 8
Longo 408

Kirkpatrick 526
Venice XIII 13, Parma XV 13
Longo 456

Allegro commodo

93

112

Kirkpatrick527
Venice XIII 14, Parma XV 14
Longo 458

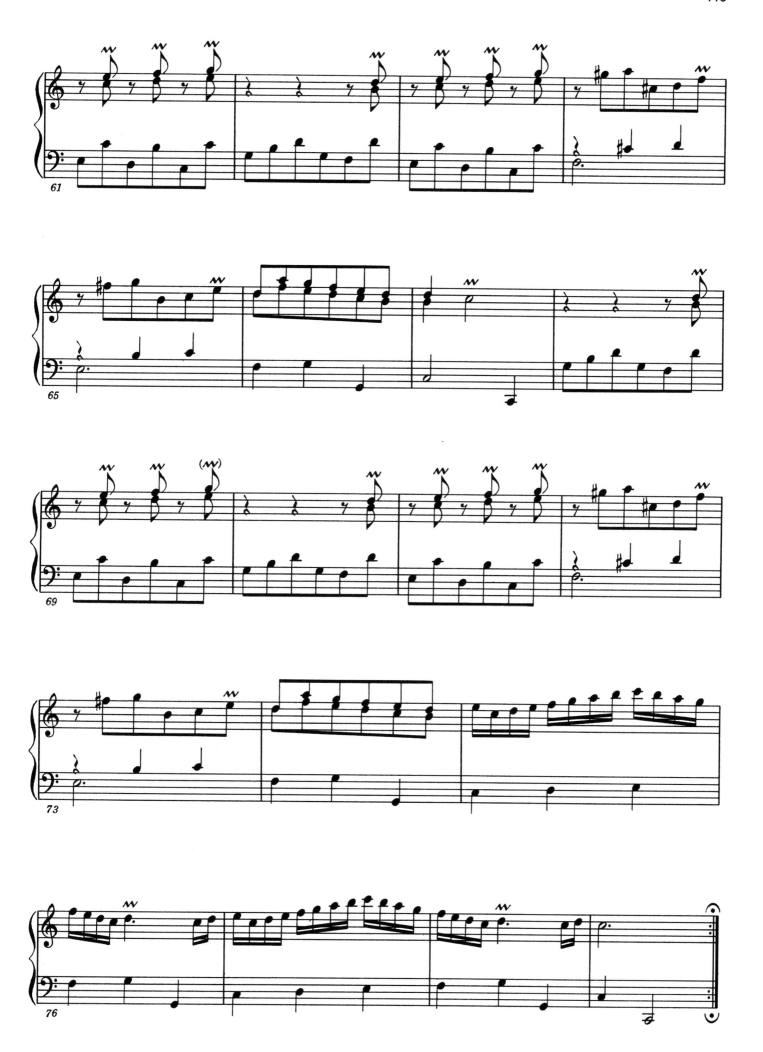

116

Kirkpatrick 532
Venice XIII 19, Parma XV19
Longo 223

118

Kirkpatrick 533
Venice XIII 20, Parma XV 20
Longo 395

Kirkpatrick 546
Parma XV 33
Longo 312

Cantabile

97

1)

Kirkpatrick 547
Parma XV 34
Longo Suppl. 28

Kirkpatrick 550
Parma XV 37
Longo Suppl. 42

Allegretto

99

Kirkpatrick551
Parma XV 38
Longo 396

END OF VOL.3

Notes on the Text of the Sonatas—Volume Three

The Venice and Parma manuscripts of the thirty-three sonatas contained in this volume are in quite similar handwriting, and we find little difference between them musically, with the single exception of Sonata No. 72. Almost all appoggiaturas and ornament signs coincide, and very few of them raise questions. In fact Nos. 68, 69, 70, 82, 84, and 89 are in perfect accord in these respects. Although my primary source with regard to appoggiaturas and ornaments has been the Parma manuscript, Nos. 72, 81, and 86 have been drawn from Venice and Nos. 79 and 92 from both manuscripts together.

When the left hand plays octave passages, and when they are written with the use of extra lower ledger lines, the tying of notes is indicated in the manuscripts only for the top part. Examples of this include Sonata No. 69 (bar 18), No. 84 (bars 80–81 and 84–85), No. 88 (bars 62–65), No. 92 (bars 64–65, 68–69, and 135–142), and No. 95 (bars 59–62, but passages between 151 and 154 are tied in both parts). There is little doubt that ties for the lower part were taken for granted, and I have added them. In the passage in Sonata No. 88, however, the bass notes, while basically the same as the others, might be repeated at the performer's discretion when the sound decays (which was not an unusual practice on the harpsichord), and thus I have used dotted lines there.

Perplexing slurs, already discussed in the Editorial Policy, Article 7, and examined in the examples of the previous two volumes, again appear in the manuscripts of the following sonatas: Nos. 70, 71, 75, 93, and 96 (Venice and Parma); 98 and 100 (Parma), where the slurs run from the first half final note of each hand and, after the page turn, lead into the second half initial note of each hand; and Nos. 85 and 89 (Venice and Parma), where the slurs appear only at the end of the first half. Considering these markings as ties across the double bar line seems to be rather impractical here, since frequently the notes are not identical or rests appear at the beginning of the second half. If we try to apply 〔1.〕〔2.〕 (that is, to skip the cadential last bar when going directly to the second half), this also creates problems, particularly when a leading tone in the penultimate bar is followed by a rest or a note of a different range at the beginning of the second half (Nos. 75, 85, 89, and 93). Examples of these situations in this volume certainly cast a strong doubt on the significance of the slurs, and unlike the two previous volumes of the present edition, I did not feel the need to cite each example individually.

Sonata No. 68 (K. 445)

1) Bar 29

I have already discussed the basic application of accidentals appearing in the manuscripts in the Editorial Policy, Article 2. Sometimes, however, we find instances where one accidental is applied to the notes which are connected under the same beam, as illustrated here (Example 1). This becomes clear by comparing with Example 2. In bar 29, therefore, I have read the left-hand third-beat last sixteenth note as $g\sharp$, the fourth-beat f as $f\natural$, and in bar 31, the right-hand second-beat second note as $g\natural''$.

Sonata No. 69 (K. 446)

1) Bar 19

Both manuscripts show ♩. ♫♩ ♪♩. :‖ ⁊ ⁊ ♪ , but I have put :‖ two beats later. Similarly, the end of this sonata: ♩. ♫♩ ♪♩. :‖ also has been revised to 〔1.〕 ♩.♫♩ ♪♩. ♩ ‖ 〔2.〕 ♩.♫♩ ♪♩.

2) Bar 21

In both Venice and Parma the left-hand seventh beat is only e', but I have added c' to match bar 23 of Parma.

3) Bar 35

In Venice the soprano sixth beat is c'''

Sonata No. 71 (K. 448)

1) Bar 37

In both manuscripts the tenor third beat is a repetition of $d\sharp'$.

Sonata No. 72 (K. 454)

The Venice version is 〔3〕♫♩ ♫♫ or ⁊ ♫ ♫♫ throughout the sonata (the figure 3 is indicated only over the first occurrence), whereas the Parma version is ♫♫ ♫♫ or ⁊ ♫ ♫♫ . Such wide discrepancies between the two sources in the notation throughout a sonata are quite unusual, especially in the later sonatas. Since Venice is smoother in the scales in bars 19–20, 24, 29, etc., I have followed it.

1) Bar 18

In Parma the third-beat *d'''* is an eighth note.

Sonata No. 74 (K. 466)

1) Bar 43

In both manuscripts the right-hand fourth-beat triplets are *c"–d♭"–e♭"*

Sonata No. 75 (K. 467)

1) Bar 102

The left-hand third-beat *b♭* is missing in both manuscripts.

Sonata No. 76 (K. 468)

1) Bar 84

In both manuscripts there appears the indication *con deto solo* (with one finger). Does this mean that a glissando is suggested? If so, how could B♭ be included in it? Sonata K. 379 in F major (not included in the present edition) bears a similar indication, but no accidental keys are called for. Here, therefore, the indication must suggest that the running scale is to be played *as though* it were a glissando.

Sonata No. 78 (K. 474)

1) Bar 46

Both Venice and Parma have the *tr* sign only here, and its position is unclear–almost between *a♮* and *e♭* . It is conceivable therefore that *tr* could apply to the *a♮* .

Sonata No. 79 (K. 475)

1) Bar 20

In Venice the left-hand first note is *d.*

2) Bar 35

The appoggiatura here and in the related phrases which follow is inconsistently indicated. In bars 35 and 39 it appears only in Parma, whereas in bar 85 only in Venice. I have used all of these and have further supplied my own in parentheses where other appoggiaturas seem to be missing.

3) Bar 71

Venice has a corona over *B♭₁.*

Sonata No. 80 (K. 478)

1) Bar 41

In both manuscripts the soprano starts at the beginning of this bar, but I have made it conform to the three previous bars.

2) Bar 70

Both Venice and Parma show *M* (left hand) directly under the third-beat *f♯'.* Since the left hand is still supposed to be holding the dotted half-note *A,* I have moved *M* to the beginning of bar 71. In bars 86–87, incidentally, *M* does not appear anywhere.

3) Bar 83

The alto half-note *e"* as well as the eighth rests are missing in both manuscripts.

Sonata No. 82 (K. 485)

1) Bar 25

In bars 25–28 and 50–53 the right-hand rhythms are quite ambiguous. For example, in Parma the first descending scale of bar 28 is [musical notation] , while in bar 51 it is [musical notation] . In Venice, bar 53, it is [musical notation] . I have unified these rhythms from one group to the next to produce at least some coherence, although in actual performance these passages could be played without adhering too much to the strict rhythm. The slurs are as indicated in the original.

Sonata No. 83 (K. 486)

1) Bar 17

The left-hand last note *g* is puzzling in both manuscripts. I have changed it to *f♯.*

2) Bar 39

Following bar 31, I have added *g'* in the alto.

Sonata No. 84 (K. 487)

1) Bar 9

In both manuscripts *tr* appears to the left of the dotted quarter-note *c",* which raises two questions: First, why is it *tr* and not ∿, and second, why is the sign not written above *e"*? It is almost impossible to play the trill on *c",* as it is likely to collide with the soprano second note, *d".* I have therefore decided that the trill should be played on the soprano *e".*

2) Bar 43

In Venice the alto third beat is *d".*

Sonata No. 85 (K. 497)

1) Bar 37

The right-hand second eighth note is *d '''* in both manuscripts, but I have changed it to *e '''* after examining bars 33 and 82.

Sonata No. 86 (K. 498)

1) Bar 58

The Parma version is as shown here, but I have followed Venice.

Sonata No. 87 (K. 499)

Parma has no tempo indication, while Venice has *And^e* .

Sonata No. 90 (K. 512)

1) Bar 4

Venice does not have the sign ᴧ here.

Sonata No. 95 (K. 532)

1) Bar 63

Sonata No. 97 (K. 546)

1) Bar 11

In Parma ᴧ is found at the beginning of bar 12, but I have changed its location to match bar 19.

Sonata No. 98 (K. 547)

1) Bar 66

The Parma notation is incorrect, and I have revised it.